Spectacular Science Projects

Janice VanCleave's

Rocks and Minerals

Mind-Boggling Experiments You Can Turn Into Science Fair Projects

John Wiley & Sons, Inc.

New York • Chichester • Brisbane • Toronto • Singapore

This text is printed on acid-free paper.

Design and production by Navta Associates, Inc.
Illustrated by Doris Ettlinger

The publisher and the author have made every reasonable effort to ensure that the
experiments and activities in this book are safe when conducted as instructed but
assume no responsibility for any damage caused or sustained while performing
the experiments or activities in this book. Parents, guardians, and/or teachers should
supervise young readers who undertake the experiments and activities in this book.

Library of Congress Cataloging-in-Publication Data
VanCleave, Janice Pratt.
    [Rocks and minerals]
    Janice VanCleave's rocks and minerals: mind-boggling experiments you can turn into
science fair projects / Janice VanCleave.
        p.   cm. —(Janice VanCleave's spectacular science projects)
    Includes index.
    ISBN 0-471-10269-5 (paper: acid-free)
    1. Rocks—Experiments—Juvenile literature. 2. Minerals—Experiments—Juvenile lit-
erature. [1. Rocks—Experiments. 2. Minerals—Experiments. 3. Science projects.
4. Experiments.] I. Title. II. Series: VanCleave, Janice Pratt. Janice VanCleave's spectacular science projects.
    QE432.2.V36   1996
    552'.0078—dc20   96–10324
                                                                                 AC

Printed in the United States of America
10 9 8 7

CONTENTS

DEDICATION

This book is dedicated to a special teacher who diligently searches for ways to make learning exciting and fun for her students. She field-tested this book with her students, and her responses were invaluable. What fun I have had exchanging ideas with my friend, Laura Fields Roberts.

ACKNOWLEDGMENTS

I would like to thank the students at Maupin Elementary in Louisville, Kentucky, for assisting me in testing the experiments in this book: Kamesha Bibbs, Daniel Bibelhauser, Ben Brown, Shaela Butler, Britney Calloway, Shawn Cheatham, Ha Dinh, Demetri Doyle, Tim Dunn, Chris Harper, Jessica Hickerson, Jeremy Hix, Megan Hix, Elizabeth Kilgore, Kevin Lam, Tiree Mason, An Nguyen, Rachel Payne, D.J. Phillips, Erin Pryor, Sarah Rainey, Tom Silva, Andre Starling, Whitney Sweeney, David Terhune, Anh Trinh, Hieu Trinh, Shaniqua Thomas, Raymond Wright, and Charles Young.

A special note of thanks to their teacher, Laura Fields Roberts, for directing the activities.

Introduction

Science is a search for answers. Science projects are good ways to learn more about science as you search for the answers to specific problems. This book will give you guidance and provide ideas, but you must do your part in the search by planning experiments, finding and recording information related to the problem, and organizing the data collected to find the answer to the problem. Sharing your findings by presenting your project at science fairs will be a rewarding experience if you have properly prepared for the exhibit.

SELECT A TOPIC

The 20 topics in this book suggest many possible problems to solve. Each topic has one "cookbook" experiment—follow the recipe and the result is guaranteed. Approximate metric equivalents have been given after all English measurements. Try several or all of these easy experiments before choosing the topic you like best and want to know more about.

KEEP A JOURNAL

Purchase a bound notebook in which you will write everything relating to the project. This is your journal. It will contain your original ideas as well as ideas you get from books or from people like teachers and scientists. It will include descriptions of your experiments as well as diagrams, photographs, and written observations of all your results. Every entry should be as neat as possible and dated. Information from this journal can be used to write a report of your project, and you will want to display the journal with your completed project. A neat, orderly journal provides a complete and accurate record of your project from start to finish. It is also proof of the time you spent sleuthing out the answers to the scientific mystery you undertook to solve.

LET'S EXPLORE

This section of each chapter follows each of 20 sample experiments and provides additional questions about the problem presented in the experiment. By making small changes to some part of the sample experiment, new results are achieved. Think about why these new results might have happened.

SHOW TIME!

You can use the format of the sample experiment to design your own experiments to solve the questions asked in "Let's Explore." Your own experiment should follow the sample experiment's format and include a single question about one idea, a list of necessary materials, a detailed step-by-step procedure, written results with diagrams, graphs, and charts if they seem helpful, and a conclusion answering and explaining the question. Include any information you found through research to clarify your answer. When you design your own experiments, make sure to get adult approval if supplies or procedures other than those given in this book are used.

If you want to make a science fair project, study the information listed here and after each sample experiment in the book to develop your ideas into a real science fair exhibit. Use the suggestions that best apply to the project topic that you have chosen. Keep in mind that while your display represents all the work that you have done, it must tell the story of the project in such a way that it attracts and holds the interest of the viewer. So keep it simple. Do not try to cram all of your information into one place. To have more space on the display and still exhibit all your work, keep some of the charts, graphs, pictures, and other materials in your journal instead of on the display board itself.

The actual size and shape of displays can be different, depending on the local science fair officials, so you will have to check the rules for your science fair. Most exhibits are allowed to be 48 inches (122 cm) wide, 30 inches (76 cm) deep, and 108 inches (274 cm) high. These are maximum measurements and your display may be smaller than this. A three-sided backboard (see drawing) is usually the best way to display your work.

Wooden panels can be hinged together, but you can also use sturdy cardboard pieces taped together to form a very inexpensive but presentable exhibit.

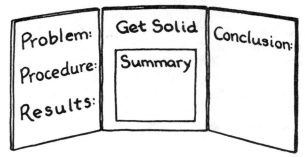

A good title of six words or less with a maximum of 50 characters should be placed at the top of the center panel. The title should capture the theme of the project but should not be the same as the problem statement. For example, if the problem under question is *How are igneous rocks formed?* a good title of the project may be "Get Solid." The title and other headings should be neat and large enough to be readable at a distance of about 3 feet (1 m). You can glue letters to the backboard (you can use precut letters that you buy or letters that you cut out of construction paper), or you can stencil the letters for all the titles. A short summary paragraph of about 100 words to explain the scientific principles involved is good and can be printed under the title. A person who has no knowledge of the topic should be able to easily understand the basic idea of the project just from reading the summary. Allow friends and adults to read the summary and ask for their reactions. Did they understand the project? It is up to you to clarify any items that need explaining.

There are no set rules about the position of the information on the display. However, it all needs to be well organized, with the title and summary paragraph as the main point at the top of the center and the remaining material placed neatly from left to right under specific headings. Choices of headings will depend on how you wish to display the information. Separate headings for Problem, Procedure, Results, and Conclusion may be used.

The judges give points for how clearly you are able to discuss the project and explain its purpose, procedure, results, and conclusion. The display should be organized so that it explains everything, but your ability to discuss your project and answer the questions of the judges convinces them that you did the work and understand what you have done. Practice a speech in front of friends, and invite them to ask you questions. If you do not know the answer to a question, never guess or make up an answer or just say, "I do not know." Instead, you can say that you did not discover that answer during your research and then offer other information that you found of interest about the project.

Be proud of the project and approach the judges with enthusiasm about your work.

OBTAINING ROCKS AND MINERALS

You may need to obtain rocks and minerals for your project. Contact the geology departments of your local colleges and universities for information. To purchase rocks and minerals that don't occur naturally in your area, check the Yellow Pages for local rock and mineral shops or teaching supply stores, or see the Appendix to this book for other sources. Chapter 20, "Collection," provides ideas for displaying a rock and mineral collection as a project. This chapter also provides helpful organization and display hints for the other projects in the book.

CHECK IT OUT!

Read about your topic in many books and magazines. You are more likely to have a successful project if you are well informed about the topic. For the topics in this book, some tips are provided about specific places to look for information. Record in your journal all the information you find, and include for each source the author's name, the book title (or magazine name and article title), the numbers of the pages you read, the publisher's name, where it was published, and the year of publication.

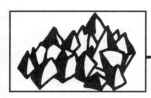

1

Building Blocks

PROBLEM

What is the difference between rocks and minerals?

Materials

3 toothpicks
6 red gumdrops (or any dark color, such as green or black)
3 white gumdrops (or any light color, such as pink or yellow)
marking pen
3 resealable plastic bags

Procedure

1. Insert 1 toothpick each in 3 of the red gumdrops.

2. Place a white gumdrop on the other end of each toothpick.

3. Label the plastic bags Mineral 1, Mineral 2, and Rock.

4. Place 2 of the remaining red gumdrops in the bag labeled Mineral 1, and 2 of the red-and-white gumdrop sets in the bag labeled Mineral 2. In the bag labeled Rock, place the last red gumdrop and the third red-and-white gumdrop set.

Results

You have made models of two different minerals and one rock.

Why?

Rocks and minerals have two things in common. First, like all materials in the universe, they are matter. **Matter** is anything that has **mass** (an amount of material) and takes up space. The building units of matter are called **atoms.** If matter is made of only one kind of atom, it is called an **element.** When two or more elements are combined, the combination of elements is called a **chemical com-**

pound. The smallest part of a chemical compound that retains the properties of the compound is called a **molecule.** Molecules consist of atoms held together by chemical bonds. Second, rocks and minerals are **solids** (phase of matter with a definite shape and a definite volume).

In the experiment, the red gumdrops represent atoms of the same element, called element 1, and the white gumdrops represent atoms of a second element called element 2. The red-and-white gumdrop sets represent molecules of a chemical compound formed by the combination of atoms of element 1 and element 2. The toothpicks represent the chemical bonds that hold atoms of the two elements together.

A **mineral** is a single solid element or chemical compound found in the earth and that has four basic characteristics. First, a mineral occurs naturally. Rubies formed in the earth are minerals, while man-made rubies are not. Second, a mineral is **inorganic** (not formed from the remains of living organisms). Diamonds are formed from pure carbon inside the earth, but coal is formed from carbon

that was once part of living things. Thus, diamonds are minerals, while coal is not. Third, each kind of mineral has a definite chemical composition, meaning the amount and kind of matter are the same for a given mineral. Fourth, each mineral has a definite structure known as a **crystal** (a solid made up of atoms arranged in an orderly, regular pattern). Perfect crystals have flat sides. Table salt is a mineral with crystals shaped like tiny cubes. The bag labeled Mineral 1 is a model of a mineral made up of element 1 atoms only. Mineral 2 is a model of a mineral made of molecules of atoms of elements 1 and 2.

Rocks are solids made up of one or more minerals, but they are not restricted to all four characteristics that describe minerals. The difference between rocks and minerals can be compared to the difference between model airplanes and the materials used to build them. Just as the building blocks of rocks are minerals, the building blocks of model airplanes are wheels, wings, propellers, and other parts. The main identifying characteristic of rocks is that they are mixtures. The model of the rock in this experiment is a mixture of an element and a chemical compound. Some rocks are granite, marble, and lava.

Rocks and minerals are the building blocks of the earth's lithosphere. The **lithosphere** includes all of the earth's **crust** (the relatively thin outermost layer of the earth) and the upper part of the earth's inner layer called the **mantle.** The lithosphere extends to a depth of about 63 miles (100 km). Thousands of different minerals have been identified in the earth's lithosphere. Only about 12 minerals are abundant and are called **rock formers** because they make up the bulk of the lithosphere.

LET'S EXPLORE

Could other rocks and minerals be formed using only two types of elements? Repeat the experiment, increasing the number of red and white gumdrops as needed. Remember that minerals contain the same element or chemical compound repeated throughout, while rocks are mixtures of different minerals. **Science Fair Hint:** Construct a display with samples of each rock and mineral model.

SHOW TIME!

Ice, which is frozen water, meets all the requirements for a mineral, but water itself does not. The symbol for water is

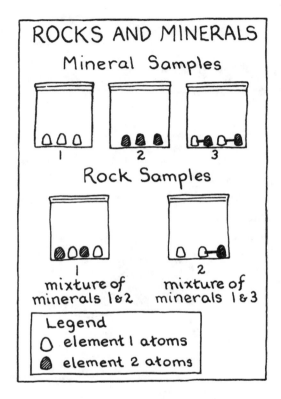

ROCKS AND MINERALS

Mineral Samples

1   2   3

Rock Samples

1   2
mixture of   mixture of
minerals 1 & 2   minerals 1 & 3

Legend
○ element 1 atoms
● element 2 atoms

water molecule loosely bonds with the hydrogen atom of another water molecule. A small flexible chain of molecules is formed. In the gas phase, fewer water molecules bond together. Ice differs from water in the liquid or gas phase in that ice is a solid with a crystalline form. The solid ice crystal is made up of water molecules, but they are bonded to form a six-sided honeycomb structure as shown in the diagram. Use gumdrops to make a model of the mineral ice. Display the gumdrop model.

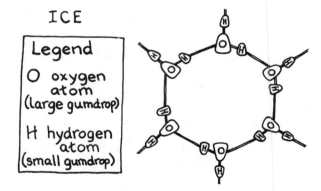

ICE

Legend
O oxygen atom
(large gumdrop)

H hydrogen atom
(small gumdrop)

H_2O, which means that each molecule of water is made up of two hydrogen (H) atoms connected to one oxygen (O) atom. Water exists as a solid, **liquid** (phase of matter with a definite volume but no definite shape), or **gas** (phase of matter with no definite volume or shape). In liquid water, the oxygen atom of one

CHECK IT OUT!

Find out more about the minerals in the earth's lithosphere. What are the names of the 12 rock-forming minerals?

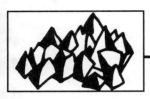

2

Patterns

PROBLEM

How do atoms and molecules arrange themselves in minerals?

Materials

large, shallow baking pan
tap water
1 teaspoon (5 ml) dishwashing liquid
spoon
drinking straw

Procedure

1. Fill the pan half full with water, then add the dishwashing liquid.

2. Gently stir with the spoon to thoroughly mix the liquids without producing any bubbles.

3. Place one end of the straw beneath the surface of the water.

4. Slowly and gently blow through the straw to make a cluster of 5 to 15 bubbles. *CAUTION: Only exhale through the straw. Do not inhale.*

5. Move the straw to a different location and blow a single bubble.

6. With the straw, move the bubble so that it touches the bubble cluster.

7. Move the straw to a different location and blow through the straw as before to make a cluster of 5 to 15 bubbles.

8. With the straw, move one bubble cluster so that it touches the other bubble cluster.

Results

The single bubble attaches to the bubble cluster. The two clusters of bubbles join, making one cluster.

Why?

The bubbles represent the chemical particles of a mineral. **Chemical particles** are the atoms or molecules that make up minerals and all matter. The addition of each bubble to the bubble cluster and the joining of the clusters represent the growth of a mineral crystal. Chemical particles, like the bubbles, can move around in a liquid. Just as a single bubble or bubble cluster moves to a place where it fits in the bubble cluster, chemical particles dissolved in a liquid move to just the right spot in order to fit with other particles. As you know, one of the four basic characteristics of minerals is that they have a definite chemical composition with atoms arranged in an orderly, regular pattern. Once a chemical particle, like the bubble, moves into the right place, it is held there by the attraction it has to the other chemical particles. This attraction between like chemical particles is called **cohesion.**

The shape and size of the chemical particles determine how they arrange themselves and the pattern they form. The orderly pattern of chemical particles gives a mineral a definite geometric shape called a crystal. Minerals exist in one of six different crystal shapes. See chapter 3, "What's Inside?" for more information about crystal shapes.

LET'S EXPLORE

Would the size of the bubbles affect the results? Repeat the experiment twice, first using a narrower straw, then replacing the straw with a cardboard tube from a paper towel roll. **Science Fair Hint:** As part of a project display, use photographs to represent the arrangement and patterns formed by the different bubble sizes.

SHOW TIME!

1a. Sugar crystals being **organic** (formed from living matter) are not minerals, but they can be used to represent the ways that crystals in minerals form. Ask an adult to prepare a sugar-gelatin solution by using the following steps:

- Pour ½ cup (125 ml) of distilled water into a small saucepan.
- Sprinkle ¼ ounce (7 g) of unfla-vored gelatin on the surface of the water and let it stand undisturbed for 2 minutes.
- Stir the liquid continuously over medium heat until the gelatin is completely dissolved.

- Slowly add 1¼ cups (313 ml) of table sugar while stirring.
- Continue to stir until all the sugar is dissolved.
- When the liquid starts to boil, remove the saucepan from the heat.
- Allow the solution to cool for 15 minutes.
- Pour the cooled solution into a 1-pint (500-ml) glass jar.

Place the jar where it can remain undisturbed for at least 2 weeks. Make daily observations and draw diagrams of the jar's contents. Display the diagrams.

b. The gelatin provided a surface for the sugar molecules to cling to. Would the molecules cling to other surfaces? Have an adult repeat the previous procedure, omitting the unflavored gelatin. Cut a piece of cotton string slightly longer than the height of the jar. Tie a paper clip to one end of the cotton string. Lower the paper clip into the jar of solution so that the paper clip rests on the bottom of the jar. Tie the free end of the string to the middle of a pencil laid across the opening of the jar. Make daily observations and diagrams of the jar's contents for at least 2 weeks.

CHECK IT OUT!

Find out more about the formation of minerals. What is a geode? How are geodes formed? What mineral is most often found in geodes?

3

What's Inside?

PROBLEM

Why are table salt crystals cube-shaped?

Materials

scissors
ruler
3 different-colored drinking straws
index card
modeling clay

Procedure

1. Cut two 1-inch (2.5-cm) pieces from each of the 3 straws, which will be referred to as straws A, B, and C.

2. Lay the index card on a table so that one short end is facing you.

3. Roll a ball of clay about the size of a marble and press it into the center of the index card. This piece of clay will be called the support stand.

4. Roll a second marble-size piece of clay. This piece of clay will be called the holder.

5. Insert about one-fourth of each piece of straw A into opposite sides of the holder.

6. Insert the free end of one of the A straws into the support stand so that both straws are perpendicular to the index card. Perpendicular means that the straws are at a 90-degree (90°) angle to the index card.

7. Insert the two pieces of straw B into opposite sides of the holder so that they are parallel to the short edges of the index card and perpendicular to the A straws.

8. Insert the two pieces of straw C into opposite sides of the holder so that they are parallel to the long edges of the index card and perpendicular to the B straws.

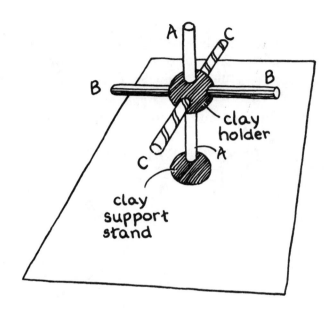

In the halite model, the different-colored straws represent these three measurements: A—height, B—width, C—length. The model represents the length of each measurement and the angle between them.

Halite is one example of a cubic crystal. Crystals are **cubic** when the combined atoms inside the crystal form a cube, or box-shaped solid having six equal, square sides that are at **right angles** (angles that measure 90°) to each other.

LET'S EXPLORE

What would the crystal look like if one of the three pairs of sides is longer? Repeat the experiment, making the length of each of the A straws 2 inches (5 cm). This is a model of a tetragonal crystal. Crystals are **tetragonal** when their atoms form a solid shaped like a rectangular shoe box or like a cube, but with a pyramid at the top and bottom. **Science Fair Hint:** Display the models of the cubic and tetragonal crystals along with mineral samples of each, such as halite for a cubic crystal and zircon or rutile for a tetragonal crystal.

Results

You have made a molecular model of **halite,** the mineral called common salt or table salt.

Why?

All minerals and many rocks are made up of crystals. Crystals, like all solids, are **three-dimensional** (having three measurements—height, width, and length).

SHOW TIME!

1. Build a paper model of a cubic halite crystal by carefully tracing the cubic pattern diagram on a sheet of typing paper. Cut the pattern out of the paper. Fold the paper along the dashed lines, making all folds in the same direction. Fold the tabs over their corresponding sides—tab A over side A, tab B over side B, and so on. Use tape to secure the tabs to the sides.

2. The mineral **zircon** has tetragonal-

CUBIC PATTERN

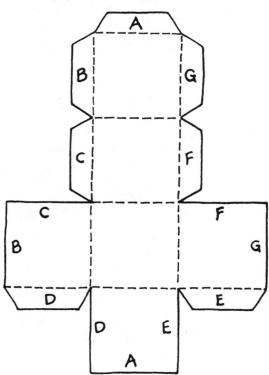

TETRAGONAL PATTERN

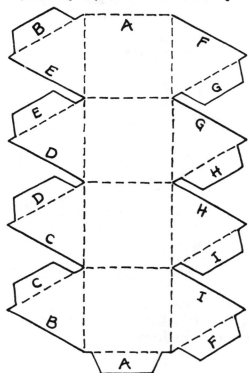

shaped crystals. Make a model of a tetragonal zircon crystal by using the previous instructions and the tetragonal pattern diagram. Create stand-up signs for this crystal model and the previous cubic model by folding an index card in half lengthwise. Label one sign Cubic (Halite) and the other Tetragonal (Zircon). Display the signs with the paper models.

CHECK IT OUT!

Cubic and tetragonal crystals are examples of two of the six common crystal systems. What are the names of all six systems? Use a rock and mineral field guide to find out more about crystal systems and mineral examples of each.

4

Snap!

PROBLEM

How do minerals break apart?

Materials

2 tablespoons (30 ml) plaster of paris
½ teaspoon (2.5 ml) white school glue
3-ounce (90-ml) paper cup
7 craft sticks or tongue depressors
2 teaspoons (10-ml) tap water
newspaper
timer

Procedure

NOTE: Mix the plaster in a throwaway container. Do not wash the container or the mixing stick in the sink, because the plaster can clog the drain.

1. Place the plaster and glue in the paper cup. Use one of the craft sticks as a mixing stick to thoroughly mix the glue and plaster.

2. Add the water to the cup. Mix thoroughly with the mixing stick.

3. Lay one of the craft sticks on the open newspaper.

4. Use the mixing stick to spread a thin layer of the plaster mixture over the surface of the stick lying on the paper.

5. Lay a second stick on top of the layer of plaster.

6. Repeat steps 4 and 5 to make a stack

of 6 sticks with plaster between each stick.

7. Allow the plaster to dry for 1 hour.

8. Hold the stack of sticks in your hands with your thumbs on the sticks that are at the top and bottom of the stack.

9. Try to pry the stack of sticks apart by pushing with your thumbs.

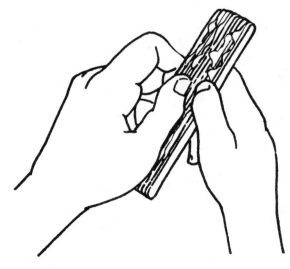

Results

The stack of sticks snaps apart, forming thinner stacks.

Why?

The stack of sticks is a model that shows how some minerals break apart. The tendency of a mineral to break along a smooth surface is called **cleavage.** A mineral may split along what is called a **cleavage plane,** which is often parallel with the face, or flat surface, of the mineral. Whether a mineral cleaves or not is determined by the arrangement of its chemical particles. In minerals with chemical particles that are strongly bonded, cleavage is difficult or does not occur at all. The weaker the bond between the particles, the more easily the mineral cleaves. Cleavage is one of the properties used in identifying minerals.

In the model, the sticks do not break when you push on them. Thus, the sticks represent areas of a mineral where the chemical particles are tightly held together. The surfaces of each stick are weakly bonded to the adjoining stick with plaster and glue, and these surfaces easily split apart when pressure is applied. These layers of plaster represent the areas of a mineral where chemical particles are weakly bonded. Thus, the model's cleavage planes are the areas between each stick.

LET'S EXPLORE

1. Produce models with greater and lesser cleavage. Repeat the experiment twice, first using 1 teaspoon (5 ml) of glue, then using no glue. The results of these experiments represent the ease of cleavage in minerals with strong and weak bonds between chemical particles along a cleavage plane.

2. Make a model with more than one cleavage direction. Repeat steps 1 through 6 in the original experiment twice to produce two stacks of sticks. Spread a layer of the plaster-glue mixture along one of the longer sides of one of the stacks. Stand the two stacks side by side with the plaster layer between the two stacks. Gently press the two stacks together, then allow to dry. **Science Fair Hint:** As part of an oral presentation of your science project, demonstrate and explain that the model can cleave in two directions because the cleavage planes are perpendicular to each other.

SHOW TIME!

1. Demonstrate the difference between cleavage and **fracture** (uneven breaking) by tearing a paper towel in half from different directions. Most brands of paper towels tear evenly from one edge, but unevenly from an adjacent edge. Try to quickly tear a paper towel from top to bottom. Try to tear another paper towel from side to side. Photographs of the results can be used to compare cleavage and fracture.

2. Collect and display minerals having different types of cleavage. See chapter 20, "Collection," for information about organizing and displaying a mineral collection.

CHECK IT OUT!

1. Use a rock and mineral handbook to find out more about cleavage. Cleavage is described as perfect, distinct, indistinct, or none. Use the handbook to determine the type of cleavage for each mineral in your display.

2. Fracture does not relate to any particular plane or direction. However, minerals that fracture do have a tendency to break apart in a certain way. Find out more about fracture. What are the different common fracture terms, and what does each type of fracture look like? Can a mineral that cleaves also fracture? Do rocks cleave and/or fracture? Add fracture type to the information card for each mineral in your display.

5

Scratch

PROBLEM

How do you determine the hardness of a mineral?

Materials

sharpened No. 2 pencil

Procedure

1. Hold the pencil against a table with one hand.

2. With your other hand, scratch the pencil lead with a fingernail.

3. Observe the ease or difficulty of making a scratch in the pencil lead.

Results

Your fingernail easily cuts a groove in the pencil lead.

Why?

Hardness is one of the most useful properties used to identify minerals. The **hardness** of a mineral is its resistance to being scratched. A hardness scale was invented in 1822 by Frederick Mohs (1773–1839), a German chemist. He arranged ten common minerals from the softest to the hardest. He gave the softest mineral, talc, the number 1, and the hardest mineral, diamond, the number 10.

The hardness value of a mineral is

determined by how easily it can be scratched when rubbed by another mineral or material of known hardness. The rule is that a mineral can scratch any mineral or material with a lower hardness number. For example, the mineral apatite, which has a hardness of 5, will scratch fluorite with a hardness of 4 or anything softer. Apatite can be scratched by orthoclase, which has a hardness of 6, or by anything harder.

Pencil lead is really not made of lead but is a mixture of the mineral graphite and clay.

Your fingernail has a hardness of about 2½. Since your nail can scratch the graphite-clay mixture in the pencil lead, the hardness of the lead must be less than 2½. Pure graphite is known to have a hardness of l, but when mixed with clay its hardness increases.

The Mohs' Hardness Scale

1. Talc
2. Gypsum
3. Calcite
4. Fluorite
5. Apatite
6. Orthoclase
7. Quartz
8. Topaz
9. Corundum
10. Diamond

LET'S EXPLORE

1. As the amount of clay mixed with graphite increases, the hardness of the pencil lead increases. Do pencil numbers correspond with the Mohs' hardness scale? That is, is a No. 1 pencil softer than a No. 2 or No. 3 pencil? Repeat the experiment twice, first using a No. 1 pencil, then using a No. 3 pencil.

2. Is gypsum harder than your fingernail? **Gypsum** is a mineral that has about the same hardness as school chalk. While chalk is not a mineral, it can be substituted for gypsum in this experiment if a sample of gypsum is not available. Repeat the original experiment, using a piece of gypsum or chalk instead of the pencil lead. If chalk is used, repeat again using different brands of chalk. Estimate the hardness of each brand. **Science Fair Hint:** Tape or glue the pencils and gypsum or chalk to poster board in order from softest to hardest. Print the estimated hardness under each sample. Use the poster as part of a project display.

3. A form of gypsum can be made by adding water to plaster of paris. Make a sample of homemade gypsum by mixing together in a paper cup 2 tablespoons (30 ml) of plaster of paris with 1 tablespoon (15 ml) of tap water. *NOTE: Do not wash plaster down the drain. It can clog the drain.* When the mixture dries (after about 20 minutes), peel off and discard the paper cup from around the solid piece of gypsum. Natural gypsum is given a rating of 2 on the Mohs' scale. How hard is your homemade gypsum? Repeat the original experiment, replacing the pencil with the homemade gypsum. Your results can determine whether the sample has a hardness of less than your fingernail, which is 2½.

SHOW TIME!

1. The hardnesses of a few everyday objects are as follows:

fingernail	2½
copper coin (penny)	3½
paper clip	4½
sandpaper	7
steel file	7½

   Make and display a chart of the Mohs' scale, similar to the one shown. On the left side of the chart, list the names of the ten minerals used for each hardness of the Mohs' scale next to their hardness number. On the right side, list the everyday objects next to their hardness number. If you like, make simple sketches or tape or glue samples of the everyday objects next to the scale. Also include the pencils and gypsum or chalk from the previous experiments and their estimated hardnesses.

2. Collect or purchase minerals to represent as many different hardnesses as possible. Using the everyday objects shown on your chart, evaluate the hardness of each mineral in your collection. Rub a sharp edge of the object whose hardness is known over the

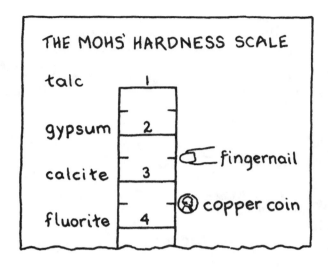

mineral to be tested. Determine whether the mineral or the object has been scratched. Estimate the hardness of the mineral. For example, if you can scratch the mineral with a paper clip but not with a copper coin, its hardness is between 3½ and 4½. A hardness of 4 would be a good estimate.

Display the mineral samples in order of their hardness. Use your hardness scale as part of the display. See chapter 20, "Collection," for suggestions on displaying a mineral collection.

6

Powdered

PROBLEM

How do you determine the streak of a mineral?

Materials

piece of gypsum
sheet of very fine sandpaper
NOTE: White school chalk is not a mineral but can be substituted for gypsum in this experiment if gypsum is not available.

Procedure

1. Rub the gypsum back and forth across the sandpaper three or four times.

2. Observe the color of the streak made by the gypsum on the sandpaper.

Results

The color of the streak is white.

Why?

The sandpaper is harder than the gypsum. Rubbing the gypsum across the

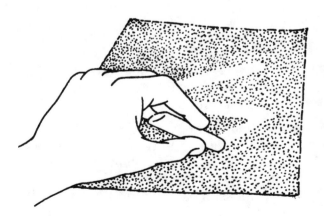

rough, hard surface of the sandpaper removes fine particles of gypsum. These particles produce the white streak on the paper. Thus, the **streak** of a mineral is the color of the powder left when the mineral is rubbed against a rough surface that is harder than the mineral. The color and the streak of gypsum are the same, but this is not true for all minerals. Since a mineral's streak can be different from its color, its streak is used for identification.

LET'S EXPLORE

1a. Gypsum is very soft and easily ground into a powder. What kind of results would you get using a harder mineral or object? Repeat the experiment, replacing the gypsum with a large paper clip. While a paper clip is not a mineral, it is harder than gypsum but softer than sandpaper.

b. Would shiny silver-colored minerals that are softer than sandpaper produce the same results? Repeat the original experiment, using samples of galena and hematite. **Science**

Fair Hint: Use a 2-by-2-inch (5-by-5-cm) square of sandpaper for the paper clip and each mineral tested. Take photographs of the objects tested, and display the photos and streaks on a poster.

SHOW TIME!

1. The color of a mineral's streak is a better clue to the identification of a mineral than is the color of the mineral itself. Rubbing a mineral across a piece of unglazed porcelain to determine the mineral's streak is called a **common streak test.** The unglazed porcelain is called a **streak plate** and has a hardness of about 7. (See chapter 5, "Scratch," for more information about a mineral's hardness.) The streak of the mineral is related to its hardness and color. The mineral must be softer than the streak plate to leave a streak. The unglazed (dull back) side of a ceramic tile can be used as a streak plate. Replace the sandpaper with this streak plate and test the streak of minerals such as pyrite and sulfur.

2. Each mineral has a specific streak color. The table shows the actual color and the streak color for a few minerals. The minerals listed were chosen for their variety of streak colors. Refer to a rock and mineral field guide for a more complete list. Using this information about minerals, make identification cards for minerals collected or purchased. Perform a streak test on the unglazed sides of separate ceramic tiles. Display the tiles, minerals, and identification cards.

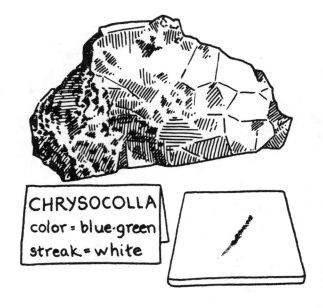

CHRYSOCOLLA
color = blue-green
streak = white

Mineral Color and Streak		
Mineral	**Color**	**Streak**
chrysocolla	green, blue, and blue-green	white
halite	colorless	white
hornblende	dark green	pale gray
limonite	yellow, brown, and black	yellow-brown

7

Heavy

PROBLEM

How do you calculate the specific gravity of a mineral?

Materials

24-inch (60-cm) piece of string
fist-size sample of quartz, or any mineral of comparable size
food scale
scissors
ruler
2-liter soda bottle
paper hole punch
flexible drinking straw
2-cup (500 ml) measuring cup
pitcher
tap water
adult helper

Procedure

1. Tie the string around the mineral.

2. Place the mineral on the scale to determine as accurately as possible its mass in grams. Record the mass.

3. Ask an adult to cut about 4 inches (10 cm) off the top of the soda bottle.

4. Use the hole punch to make a hole about 1 inch (2.5 cm) from the rim of the bottle.

5. Insert about ½ inch (1.25 cm) of the flexible end of the straw in the hole.

6. Bend the straw so that it forms a 90° angle. Place the measuring cup under the free end of the straw.

7. Use the pitcher to pour water into the bottle until it is just above the straw. Water will flow through the straw and into the cup.

8. When the water stops flowing into the cup, empty the cup. Replace the empty cup, then; holding the mineral

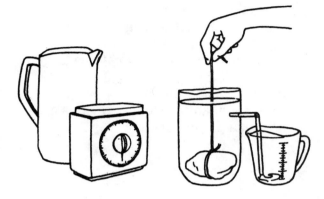

by the string, slowly lower it into the bottle. Do not let the water spill over the rim of the bottle.

9. When the water stops flowing into the measuring cup, record the amount of water in the cup in milliliters. This is the amount, in milliliters, of water **displaced** (pushed out of place) by the mineral.

10. Use the following example to determine the specific gravity (S.G.) of your mineral specimen:

Example:

A mineral with a mass of 150 grams displaces 60 milliliters of water.

- **specific gravity (S.G.)** = mass of mineral divided by mass of water displaced by the mineral
- mass of mineral = 150 g
- volume of displaced water = 60 ml
- 1 ml of water has a mass of 1 g so the mass of displaced water = 60 g

S.G. = 150 g ÷ 60 g

= 2.5

Results

The specific gravity of the mineral in the example is 2.5.

Why?

Specific gravity is the ratio of the mass of a substance, such as a mineral, in air compared to the mass of an equal volume of water. To calculate specific gravity, divide the mass of the mineral by the mass of the water displaced by the mineral. The answer tells you how many times heavier the mineral is than water. The mineral in the example is 2.5 times as heavy as water. Most minerals have a specific gravity greater than 1, meaning that they are heavier than water. Every mineral has a certain specific gravity, thus the specific gravity of a mineral can be used as a clue to its identity.

LET'S EXPLORE

1. Would a different piece of quartz of the same size have the same specific gravity? Repeat the experiment, using a different piece of quartz of about the same size.

2. Does the size of the mineral affect the results? Repeat the original experiment twice, first using a smaller sample of the mineral, then using a larger sample of the mineral. **Science Fair Hint:** Use the mineral samples and their calculated specific gravities as part of a project display.

SHOW TIME!

Use the following steps for another method to determine specific gravity:
- Tie a string around a mineral and hang it from a spring scale. Record this as weight 1.

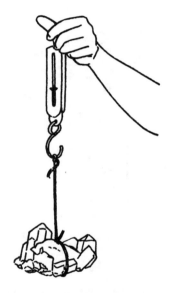

- Fill a large bowl half full with water.
- With the mineral hanging from the scale, lower the mineral into the water. Record this as weight 2.
- Subtract weight 2 from weight 1. Record the answer as weight 3.

- Divide weight 1 by weight 3 to get the mineral's specific gravity.

CHECK IT OUT!

Diamond and graphite both are made from carbon. The specific gravity of diamond is 3.5, while that of graphite is only 2.3. They differ in specific gravity because they differ in how the carbon atoms combine. Find out more about the specific gravity of different minerals. Make a list of the specific gravity of as many minerals as possible.

8

Bubbler

PROBLEM

How can you identify carbonates?

Materials

long-handled spoon
raw egg
quart (liter) wide-mouthed glass jar
1 quart (1 liter) white vinegar

Procedure

1. Use the spoon to place the egg in the jar, being careful not to crack the egg.

2. Fill the jar with vinegar.

3. Observe the eggshell immediately and then periodically for the next 2 days.

Results

Bubbles start forming immediately on the surface of the eggshell and increase in number over time. After about 2 days,

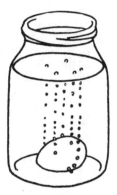

the shell is no longer present, and a thin membrane holds the egg together.

Why?

The main ingredient of the eggshell is calcium carbonate. When calcium carbonate combines with an acid, such as vinegar, it dissolves as new materials are produced, including carbon dioxide gas. The bubbles seen rising in the jar are carbon dioxide gas.

Minerals containing combinations

of carbon and oxygen and some other element, such as calcium, barium, or manganese, are called **carbonates.** Carbonates can be identified by the fact that they, like the eggshell, produce bubbles of carbon dioxide gas when combined with an acid. Some carbonates require a very strong acid to produce carbon dioxide gas but many react with weaker acids, such as vinegar.

The most common carbonate is **calcite,** which contains calcium carbonate. Calcite, like most carbonates, tends to be fairly soft. It has a hardness of 3, cleaves perfectly in three different directions, is usually whitish or colorless, and has a white to grayish streak. The rocks limestone and marble are made from calcite.

LET'S EXPLORE

Some types of school chalk are a form of calcium carbonate mixed with a clay binder, while other types are made mostly of gypsum (a mineral made of calcium sulfate). Strong acids will cause the gypsum to bubble, but weak acids, such as vinegar, will cause little or no reaction. Even weak acids, however, will cause calcium carbonate to produce large amounts of bubbles. Collect different brands of school chalk to identify which contain calcium carbonate and which contain gypsum. Repeat the experiment, using a baby food jar filled with vinegar and a small piece of chalk instead of the egg. Perform the experiment for each chalk sample. The presence of many bubbles means the chalk contains calcium carbonate, but if there are few to no bubbles, the chalk is made from some other material, such as gypsum.

SHOW TIME!

1. You can identify calcium carbonate without allowing the sample to totally dissolve by removing the chalk as soon as you determine whether or not a carbonate is present. Do this by tying a 12-inch (30-cm) piece of string around each piece of chalk. Lower one piece of chalk into the jar of vinegar. Wait 5 to 10 seconds, or as soon as bubbles are seen, then remove the chalk from the vinegar. Rinse the chalk in water. Test each of the chalk pieces using this method. Record your observations on a chart similar to the one shown.

Chalk sample	Observation	Carbonate (yes or no)
1		
2		
3		

2. For soft minerals, use the edge of a spoon to scrape some of the mineral into a mound on a saucer. Add 2 to 3 drops of vinegar to the mound of powder. Use this method to test for the presence of calcium carbonate in

school chalk. Also test soft minerals such as talc and gypsum.

3. A more common method of identifying a carbonate is to use an eyedropper to add a few drops of acid, such as vinegar, to the mineral sample being tested. Choose a spot on the sample that is not particularly interesting, as acid may damage the surface. After 5 to 10 seconds or as soon as the bubbles are seen collecting on the surface of the sample, you can rinse off the acid with water.

CHECK IT OUT!

The most common carbonate, calcite, contains $CaCO_3$, calcium carbonate. The mineral witherite contains $BaCO_3$, barium carbonate. Use a rock and mineral field guide to find out more about the names of different carbonates and the carbonate compounds they contain.

9

Pointer

PROBLEM

How can you make a mock magnetic mineral?

Materials

½ teaspoon (2.5 ml) iron filings (found at teaching supply stores)
1 teaspoon (5 ml) plaster of paris
3-ounce (90-ml) paper cup
eyedropper
tap water
craft stick
bar magnet
12-inch (30-cm) piece of thread
transparent tape
compass

Procedure

NOTE: Mix the plaster in a throwaway container. Do not wash the container or the craft stick in the sink, because the plaster can clog the drain.

1. Add the iron filings and plaster of paris to the cup. Mix thoroughly.

2. Add the water, 10 drops at time, and stir with the craft stick. Continue to add water and stir until the mixture forms a paste thick enough to be shaped. It will take about 40 to 50 drops of water.

3. Remove the paste from the cup and shape it into a cylinder about 1 inch (1.25 cm) long.

4. Center the cylinder inside the cup.

5. Stand the cup on one end of the magnet with the ends of the cylinder in line with the ends of the magnet.

6. Leave the cup undisturbed until the plaster cylinder inside dries. This should take about 15 to 20 minutes.

7. Make a slipknot in one end of the thread by following the steps in the diagram, folding end A over end B

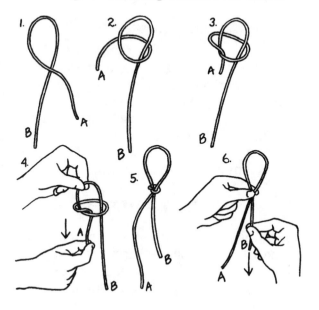

and looping the thread as shown. In step 4, hold the loop and pull end A to tighten the knot. In step 6, hold the knot and pull end B to reduce the size of the loop. Be careful not to pull end B too tightly, or the slip-knot may come undone.

8. Remove the plaster cylinder from the cup and insert it in the loop of the knot, then tighten the loop securely around the cylinder.

9. Tape the free end of the thread to the edge of a table.

10. Allow the plaster cylinder to hang freely. *NOTE: Make sure that the magnet is not near the table.*

11. Hold the compass at a distance and determine the direction to which the cylinder points.

Results

The cylinder dries, forming a gray solid with reddish spots throughout. It hangs in a north-to-south direction.

Why?

All materials are made up of tiny bits of matter called atoms. In magnetic mate-

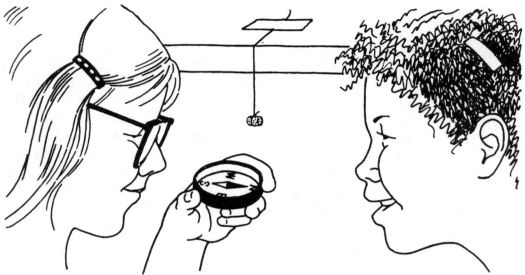

rials, clusters of atoms called **magnetic domains** organize themselves so that one side of the cluster is attracted to the earth's magnetic north pole and the other side is attracted to the earth's magnetic south pole. When many of the domains line up so that their north-seeking sides point in the same direction, the material is said to be **magnetized.**

When you place the plaster cylinder near the magnet, the domains in the iron filings line up with the **poles** (ends) of the magnet. Thus, the plaster cylinder becomes magnetized and behaves in a way similar to **magnetite,** a magnetic mineral containing a high percentage of iron. Magnetite is also called **lodestone** ("leading stone"), because it acts like a compass if a piece of the stone is suspended from a thread. The plaster cylinder is a model of mock magnetite.

LET'S EXPLORE

Would the amount of iron in mock magnetite affect its magnetic properties? Repeat the experiment twice, first using ¼ teaspoon (1.3 ml) of iron filings, then

using 1 teaspoon (5 ml) of iron filings.
Science Fair Hint: Mark the north-facing end of the stone with a pen. Lay a support beam across the top of your project display frame. Hang the mock magnetite from the beam so that you can demonstrate its ability to point in the direction of the earth's magnetic north pole.

SHOW TIME!

1. Purchase a piece of magnetite from a rock and mineral shop or catalog supplier and test its magnetic properties by suspending it from a thread. Use a compass to determine the direction north and place a small piece of tape on the north-pointing side of the stone. Move the hanging stone from place to place to determine whether the taped side continues to seek out the earth's magnetic north pole.

2. Magnetite was used in ancient times to make compass needles. Use your mock magnetite to make your own compass needle. Lay the stone on a table and place a sewing needle on top of the stone so that the point of the needle points toward the north-seeking end of the stone (the end with the pen mark). After 2 minutes, remove the needle and ask an adult to weave it through the center of a 1-inch (2.5-cm) -square piece of paper. Place the paper in the center of a bowl of water. *NOTE: Make sure that there are no magnets near the bowl.* Use a real compass to determine which way your floating compass needle is pointing. Display your floating compass needle with the real compass.

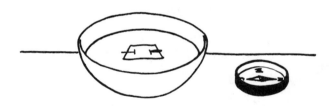

CHECK IT OUT!

Lodestone is mentioned in ancient writings and is sometimes called *magnete stone* after a Greek tribe, the Magnetes. This tribe lived in the district of Magnesia, in Asia Minor, where large deposits of lodestone were found. Find out more about magnetite. Besides being magnetic, what are its other identifying characteristics, such as color, hardness, and streak? How is it used? Where is it found?

Dripstones

PROBLEM

What are stalactites and stalagmites?

Materials

1 cup (250 ml) Epsom salts
two 5-ounce (150-ml) paper cups
tap water
spoon
10-inch (25-cm) piece of cotton string
2 paper clips
6-by-10-inch (15-by-25-cm) piece of
   cardboard
timer

Procedure

1. Pour ½ cup (125 ml) of Epsom salts
into each paper cup.

2. Add just enough water to cover the
Epsom salts in each cup.

3. Stir. Most of the Epsom salts will not
dissolve.

4. Thoroughly wet the cotton string with
water, then run the string between your
thumb and index finger to remove the
excess water from the string.

5. Tie a paper clip to each end of the
string, then place 1 paper clip in each
cup.

6. Set the cups on the cardboard and
position them so that the center of the
string hangs about 1 inch (2.5 cm)
above the cardboard.

7. Place the cups in a draft-free area
where they will not be disturbed.

8. Observe the string every 5 minutes

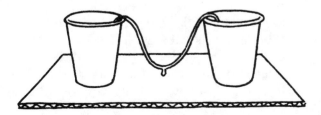

for a half an hour, then every 24 hours for 7 days. Record your observations.

Results

Usually within 5 minutes, a drop of liquid forms and hangs from the center of the string. This drop falls and another drop forms. This occurs several times during the first 30 minutes. After 24 hours, the drop begins to look like ice, and icy-looking crystals are seen on the cardboard beneath the string. After 7 days, a white frosty crust has formed that hangs from the string. In addition, a mound of white crystals builds up on the cardboard beneath the string. *NOTE: If this does not happen, see the variations in "Let's Explore."*

Why?

Water containing Epsom salts moves through the string. As the water evaporates, frosty crystals of Epsom salts are deposited along the string and hang down from its center. A small mound of white crystals also forms on the cardboard. The formation of these hanging crystals and the crystal mound demonstrates the way mineral deposits form in caves.

The long hanging spikes in caves form when rainwater containing carbon dioxide from the air combines with **limestone** (a rock made wholly or chiefly of calcium carbonate). As this liquid seeps through the roofs of caves, small particles of calcium carbonate, generally in the form of calcite, cling to the ceiling. The calcite deposits build up, eventually forming long hanging spikes called **stalactites.** Drops of liquid that splash to the floor of the cave leave calcite deposits over a wide area. As more drops land, a rounded deposit builds upward. Mounds of calcite projecting up from a cave floor are called **stalagmites.** Stalactites and stalagmites are commonly called **dripstones.**

LET'S EXPLORE

1. **Humidity** (the amount of water in the air) in caves can be high. Can humidity affect the growth of the crystals? Repeat the experiment during times of high, moderate, and low humidity. The local weather report on TV or radio or in your newspaper will give the current level of humidity.

2. Does the length of the string affect the results? Repeat the original experiment, using a string 24 inches (60 cm) long.

3. Does the height from which the drops fall affect the results? Repeat the variation of the experiment that works best, but this time set the cups on boxes to raise the string at least 6 inches (15 cm) above the cardboard. **Science Fair Hint:** Take photographs daily of this and the previous experiments. Use the photos to prepare display posters comparing the results of each experiment. The figure shows one method of arranging the photographs.

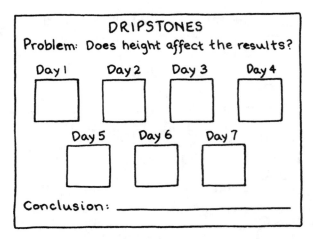

SHOW TIME!

1a. Further demonstrate how high humidity affects the growth of the crystals by preparing the cups as in the original experiment. Place the cups at each end of a see-through plastic storage box. Pour enough water into the box to cover the bottom with a thin layer of water. Cut a string long enough so that it reaches between the cups and hangs about 1 inch (2.5 cm) above the water's surface. Tie a washer to each end of the string. Wet the string as before, then place one washer in each cup. Cut a piece of black construction paper to cover a saucer, then place the saucer under the center of the string. Place the lid on the box. Set the box where it will not be disturbed. Observe the string every day for 7 days. Make daily drawings to use as part of the project display.

b. Demonstrate low humidity by repeating the above procedure, but replace the water with borax (a powdered water softener found at the grocery store). Borax will absorb water from the air, making the air around the string dry.

2. Caves are usually cool. In addition to humidity, does temperature affect the growth of the crystals? Repeat the previous experiments, preparing two boxes, a high-humidity box with water and a low-humidity box with borax. This time, place the boxes in a section of the refrigerator where they will not be disturbed. Carefully remove the boxes and make observations once a week for 2 to 3 weeks.

CHECK IT OUT!

1. Dripstones are also called *speleothems,* from two Greek words meaning "set down in caves." Use earth science texts and encyclopedias to find out more about speleothems. What are the shapes of speleothems that are called columns, soda straws, helicitites, flowstone, and cave pearls? How are these structures formed?

2. The calcium carbonate in speleothems is generally in the form of the mineral calcite. Sometimes the calcium carbonate forms aragonite crystals. Find out more about calcite and aragonite. How do these minerals differ? What is the difference in the appearance of speleothems formed by these minerals? What type of formations in caves are produced by other minerals, such as gypsum and epsomite?

11

Sliced

PROBLEM

How can you make a model of a slice of a rock?

Materials

scissors
ruler
4 sheets of construction paper—
    yellow, pink, white, and black
glue

Procedure

1. Cut one square from each sheet of construction paper in the following sizes:
   - yellow—5 × 5 inches (12.5 × 12.5 cm)
   - pink—4 × 4 inches (10 × 10 cm)
   - white—2 × 2 inches (5 × 5 cm)
   - black—1 × 1 inch (2.5 × 2.5 cm)

2. Cut each square except the yellow one into the number and shape of pieces shown:
   - pink—16 equal squares
   - white—24 equal rectangles
   - black—8 equal triangles

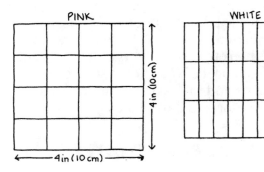

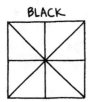

3. Glue all of the paper pieces to the yellow paper in a random pattern. Cover as much of the yellow paper as possible.

Results

You've created a model of a slice of the rock granite.

Why?

Rocks are identified by the minerals they contain. Granite is a rock made up of a mixture of minerals, mainly feldspar, quartz, and mica. Hornblende may also be present. In all samples of granite, each of these minerals look similar except for their colors. Feldspar is often pink or white. Quartz can be clear, gray, pink, or white and is always glassy looking. Mica is generally dark gray to black.

The paper pieces in the model of granite represent the minerals feldspar (pink paper), quartz (white paper), and mica (black paper). The yellow represents hornblende or any other mineral that may be present. Because the model contains a high percentage of pink feldspar, it represents pink granite. Granite samples made up of the same minerals may

Legend
■ pink (feldspar)
□ white (quartz)
▲ black (mica)

look different because they contain different amounts and sizes of each mineral. The model represents a smooth slice cut from a piece of pink granite, but the actual rock would be rough with coarse grains of minerals.

LET'S EXPLORE

1. Different slices cut from the same piece of granite may look very different. Demonstrate this by repeating the experiment, but this time have a helper arrange the pieces in a random pattern without looking at your model.

2. All pieces of pink granite do not contain the same amount of each mineral. Repeat the original experiment, cutting the same number and shape of pieces from each color of paper, but using these measurements for each color:
- 1 yellow (hornblende) square—5 × 5 inches (12.5 × 12.5 cm)
- 16 pink (feldspar) squares—5 × 4 inches (12.5 × 10 cm)
- 24 white (quartz) rectangles—1 × 2 inches (2.5 × 5 cm)
- 8 black (mica) triangles—½ × ½ inch (1.25 × 1.25 cm)

3. All pieces of granite do not have the same color. Make a model of white granite by repeating the original experiment, using these quantities, colors, shapes, and measurements.
- 1 yellow (hornblende) square—5 × 5 inches (12.5 × 12.5 cm)

- 16 white (feldspar) squares—4 × 4 inches (10 × 10 cm)
- 24 light gray (quartz) rectangles—2 × 2 inches (5 × 5 cm)
- 8 black (mica) triangles—1 × 1 inch (2.5 × 2.5 cm)

SHOW TIME!

1a. Produce a mock sample of granite. Mix the following colors and amounts of aquarium gravel together in a 3-ounce (90-ml) paper cup:
- pink—1 tablespoon (15 ml)
- white—1 teaspoon (5 ml)
- any dark color—½ teaspoon (2.5 ml)

Add 1 teaspoon (5 ml) of white school glue and mix thoroughly with a craft stick. Allow the cup to sit for 24 hours or until the glue is dry.

b. Make different mock samples of pink granite by repeating the previous experiment using different amounts of pink gravel. The mock rocks can be removed from their cups and displayed. Label each rock Mock Pink Granite.

2. Purchase a piece of granite from a rock and mineral shop or catalog supplier. Use a magnifying lens to observe the surface of the rock. Make and display colored drawings of several magnified views of the rock.

CHECK IT OUT!

Granite is a type of rock formed when hot liquid rock beneath the earth's surface cools and hardens. Use an earth science text to find out more about granite. How is granite used? What is an igneous rock?

12

Squeezed

PROBLEM

How is sedimentary rock formed?

Materials

2 standard-size bed pillows with
   covers removed
marking pen
1-inch (2.5-cm) piece of masking tape
ruler
helper

Procedure

1. Fluff the pillows to make them as large as possible.

2. Lay 1 pillow on a table with its longer side facing you.

3. Draw an arrow lengthwise on the piece of tape.

4. Hold the tape so that the arrow is parallel to the tabletop. Stick the tape in the middle of the side of the pillow facing you.

5. Use the ruler to measure the distance from the tabletop to the arrow on the piece of tape.

6. Ask your helper to gently lower the second pillow on top of the first one. Again, read the measurement on the ruler.

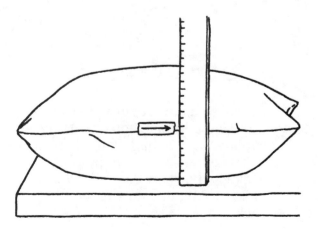

Results

The height of the bottom pillow decreased when the second pillow was placed on top.

Why?

Sedimentary rock is formed by deposits of **sediment** (small particles of material carried and deposited by wind, water, or ice). Sediment can be bits of shells, rocks, or the hardened remains of plants and animals. After thousands of years, thick layers of sediment can build up.

The pillows in this experiment each represent a layer of sediment. In order for sediments to form rock, they must be held together. The squeezing process of **compaction** is one way in which sediments are held together. Over time, sediments become compacted because the weight of upper layers of sediment squeeze the lower layers of sediment closer together, in the same way that the second pillow squeezed the first pillow. Sedimentary rock forms when the layers of sediment harden.

LET'S EXPLORE

1. Would larger pillows affect the results? Repeat the experiment, using queen- or king-size pillows.

2. Would the number of pillows affect the results? Repeat the original experiment, using four or more pillows.

3. How does time affect the results? Repeat the original experiment, using at least four pillows. Measure and record the height of the bottom pillow on a chart similar to the one shown. Continue to measure the height of the pillow at set intervals, such as after 2, 6, 12, 24, and 48 hours. *NOTE: Be sure to place the pillows where they will not be disturbed.*

Height of Lower Sediment Layer

Time, in hours	Height, in inches (cm)
0 (start)	
2	
6	
12	
24	
48	

SHOW TIME!

1a. Another way in which sediments are held together is **cementation** (the process by which minerals dissolved in water cement sediments together). Demonstrate that water usually contains dissolved minerals by placing a 2-inch (5-cm) -square section of a clear, colorless plastic report folder or a small piece of clear plastic food wrap near a window. Add enough tap water to make a small pool of water in the center of the plastic. Do not disturb the plastic until the water **evaporates** (changes from a liquid to a gas). Then hold the plastic up to the light and examine the material left on the plastic.

b. Does the amount of dissolved minerals in water differ from one place to the next? Determine the answer by repeating the previous experiment, using samples of tap water from different areas. These water samples can be collected during a vacation and/or from friends who live in different parts of the country. Label the plastic pieces with the

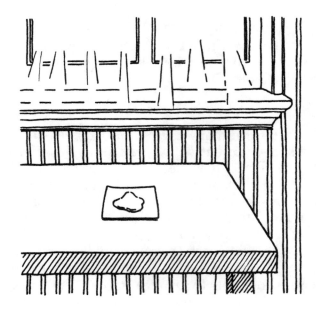

area that the water sample came from, and use them as part of your project display.

2. Water in the lower squeezed layers of sediment contains dissolved minerals picked up as the water passed through the upper sediment layers. Demonstrate this process by filling a large paper cup half full with sand, then fill the cup with soil. Use a pencil point to punch 3 to 4 small holes in the bottom of the cup. Hold the

cup above a clean jar as a helper slowly pours about ½ cup (125 ml) of distilled water into the cup. Repeat the previous experiment, using this collected water.

CHECK IT OUT!

Sedimentary rock can be divided into clastic and nonclastic rocks. Clastic rocks are classified according to the size and shape of the rock pieces they contain. Nonclastic rocks are made of two types, chemical rocks and organic rocks. Use an earth science text and/or a science encyclopedia to find out more about sedimentary rock. How does the formation of clastic and nonclastic rocks differ? How are nonclastic rocks classified? What are the different clastic and nonclastic classifications?

13

Recycled Rock

PROBLEM

How is metamorphic rock formed?

Materials

newspaper
two 12-by-12-inch (30-by-30-cm) sheets
   of waxed paper
2 slices of dark bread
1 slice of white bread
scissors

Procedure

1. Lay several sheets of newspaper on the floor.

2. Place 1 sheet of waxed paper on top of the newspaper.

3. Put the 3 slices of bread together so that the white slice is sandwiched between the 2 dark slices.

4. Lay the bread sandwich on the first sheet of waxed paper.

5. Place the second sheet of waxed paper on top of the sandwich.

6. Walk back and forth several times across the waxed paper that covers the sandwich.

7. Remove the sandwich and cut it in half with scissors.

8. Observe the cut edges of the sandwich.

Results

Three thin layers of bread are formed, two dark layers with a white layer between them.

Why?

The three slices of the bread sandwich represent three layers of sedimentary rock. When you apply pressure to this model of sedimentary rock by walking back and forth across it, the model changes into that of another type of rock called metamorphic rock. **Metamorphic rock** is rock that forms from other types of rock by pressure and heat. This process of changing from one rock type to another is called **metamorphism.**

Metamorphism occurs at great depths within the earth's crust or at other areas of high pressure and temperature.

During metamorphism, the original rock stays in solid form, but bits of material making up the rock are pushed around and **compressed** (squeezed closer together). This changes the size and arrangement of the mineral grains in the rock.

LET'S EXPLORE

1. Would more or less pressure on the sandwich affect the results? Repeat the experiment twice. First, ask someone who weighs less than you to walk across the sandwich. Then, ask someone who weighs more than you to perform the experiment. For best results, choose people much lighter and much heavier than yourself.

2. The greatest amount of metamorphism occurs close to the center of mountain building, deep within the earth. These are areas of very high pressure and temperature. Demonstrate this pressure and movement of rocks by repeating the original experiment, but this time stand with the back of the heel of your shoe on the

sandwich, and the toe of your shoe up. Shift your weight to this heel, then twist your foot back and forth several times. Push the heel of your foot as hard as possible against the bread, squishing the bread under your heel. **Science Fair Hint:** Keep all of the models produced and use them as part of a project display. Place the models in sealed plastic bags. Label each bag Low-, Moderate-, or High-Pressure Metamorphism, depending on the amount of pressure applied to the bread.

SHOW TIME!

1. Metamorphism also occurs at great depths beneath the earth's surface. The weight of rock layers above compress the rock below, crushing individual mineral grains and flattening them. Make a model of this restructuring of mineral crystals. Snap about 20 flat toothpicks in the middle without breaking them apart. Place the bent toothpicks in a bowl and use your hands to mix the toothpicks. Then,

pour the toothpicks onto a table. Place a heavy book on top of the toothpicks and press down. Remove the book, and observe that many of the toothpicks, like mineral crystals, are crushed and flattened as a result of compression.

2. Metamorphic rocks are classified as either **foliated rocks** (rocks with layers) or **nonfoliated rocks** (rocks without layers). Use an earth science text to find out more about these two classifications. Prepare a classification chart for metamorphic rocks using foliated and nonfoliated as main divisions. List rocks, major features, and major minerals.

CHECK IT OUT!

Metamorphic rock is solid rock that remains in a solid state while it changes in both composition and texture. If melting and rehardening occur, however (as happens beneath the earth's surface), the rock is not considered metamorphic but is called igneous rock. Find out more about metamorphic rock. What is the temperature range that allows these rocks to form without being melted? At what depths do the rocks form?

14

Melt Down

PROBLEM

Can solid rock melt?

Materials

cup
warm tap water
spoon
timer
½-by-½-inch (1.25-by-1.25 cm) square of
   milk chocolate candy
saucer
toothpick

Procedure

1. Fill the cup with warm tap water.

2. Place the spoon in the cup of water.

3. After about 30 seconds, remove the spoon from the water and place the chocolate in the spoon.

4. Set the spoon on the saucer.

5. Use the toothpick to move the chocolate around in the spoon.

Results

The chocolate melts.

Why?

Chocolate is solid at room temperature, but like all solids, it melts when heated, forming a liquid. The temperature at which a solid changes to a liquid is called its **melting point.** Because chocolate has a low melting point, the heat from the spoon is enough to raise the chocolate's temperature to the melting point. The hotter the chocolate gets, the more **fluid** (capable of flowing) it becomes.

The change in the chocolate from a solid to a liquid due to an increase in its temperature is similar to the change of solid rock to **magma** (liquid rock beneath the earth's surface). Rocks have a much higher melting point than the chocolate. The tremendous heat at depths of about 25 to 37½ miles (40 to 60 km)

below the earth's surface is great enough to melt rock. As with chocolate, the hotter magma is, the more fluid it is. Sometimes blocks of solid rock above a pool of magma break off and fall into the magma. If the temperature of the magma is below the melting point of these fallen rocks, they remain as solid chunks. These solid pieces of rock mixed with the molten (melted) rock are called **xenoliths.**

LET'S EXPLORE

1. Does all candy melt at the same temperature? Repeat the experiment, using different kinds of candy, such as caramel, white chocolate, and peppermint. **Science Fair Hint:** Use the results as part of a report to explain that rocks, like candy, do not all melt at the same temperature. Mention that although all rocks do not melt at the same temperature, they all eventually melt and form magma beneath the earth's surface because of the extreme heat. Magma has a temperature usually between 1,022°F and 2,192°F (550°C and 1,200°C).

2. What happens when magma cools slowly? Repeat the original experiment, but this time continue to move the chocolate with the toothpick for 1 minute or until it no longer moves easily. The resulting solid represents **igneous rock** (rock formed when hot liquid rock cools and hardens), formed by slow cooling magma beneath the earth's surface. See chapter 15, "Transformed," for more information about igneous rock.

3. What happens when magma rises to the surface and cools quickly? Magma that reaches the earth's surface is called **lava.** Demonstrate the quick cooling of lava by filling a glass with ice and water. Then repeat the original experiment, but place the spoon with the melted chocolate in the glass of ice water. After about 10 seconds, remove the spoon and touch the candy with your finger. The chocolate has become solid again. This solidified chocolate represents igneous rock formed by the quick cooling of lava.

SHOW TIME!

1. Magma is a thick liquid. Thick liquids are said to have a high **viscosity** (the property of a liquid that makes it

resistant to flow). Liquids such as water, honey, and shampoo can be used to represent magma of various viscosities. Test the viscosity of each liquid by placing 1 drop of each liquid about 2 inches (5 cm) apart on a metal baking pan. Then slowly raise the end of the pan until one of the drops starts to move down the pan. The slower the movement of the drop of liquid, the more viscous (resistant to flow) the liquid is.

2. Demonstrate the effect of temperature on the viscosity of magma by repeating the previous experiment twice. The first time, raise the temperature of the samples before performing the experiment. To do this, place 1 tablespoon (15 ml) of each sample in separate baby food jars. Set the jars in a bowl. Pour warm water into the bowl to a height greater than that of the liquids in the jars. Wait 3 minutes, stir the liquids, then perform the experiment. The second time, begin by lowering the temperature of the samples. Place the jars containing the remaining unused samples in the refrigerator for about 30 minutes, then perform the experiment. Use diagrams and the

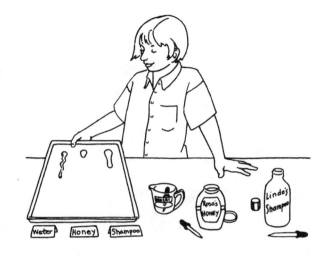

results of each experiment as part of a project display.

CHECK IT OUT!

The three principal kinds of magma are andesitic, basaltic, and rhyolitic. Find out more about the characteristics of these magma types. What is their chemical composition? How does the viscosity of each differ? For more information about magma, see "Up and Down" on pages 16–19 in *Janice VanCleave's Volcanoes* (New York: Wiley, 1994).

15

Transformed

PROBLEM

How is igneous rock formed?

Materials

strainer large enough to fit across the
   bowl
deep bowl
2 sheets of construction paper—
   1 yellow, 1 blue
food blender (to be used only by an
   adult)
2 cups (500 ml) tap water
1 teaspoon (15 ml) white school glue
timer
10 to 12 sheets of newspaper
adult helper

Procedure

1. Set the strainer across the mouth of
   the bowl.

2. Tear each sheet of construction paper
   into 16 pieces: tear the sheet in half,
   then placing the torn pieces together
   and tear them again. Repeat this 2
   more times.

3. Drop the paper pieces into the blender.

4. Add the water and glue to the blender.

5. Ask an adult to turn on the blender and
   thoroughly mix the paper and water. A
   thick paper mulch will be produced.

6. Pour the paper mulch into the strainer
   over the bowl, and let it sit undisturbed for about 20 minutes.

7. When 20 minutes have passed, fold
   the newspaper sheets in half and lay
   them on the table. Pick up the wet
   paper mulch with your hand and place
   it on top of the newspaper.

8. Allow the paper mulch to dry and
   solidify. This may take 2 to 3 days.

Results

The dark greenish gray mulch becomes a lumpy solid.

Why?

The blending of different-colored paper pieces and water represents the melting of different rocks beneath the surface of the earth due to heat and pressure. This melted rock is called magma. When magma rises to the surface of the earth, it is then called lava. Magma and lava cool and solidify to form a type of rock called igneous rock. The drying of the paper mulch represents the cooling of magma or lava to form igneous rock.

LET'S EXPLORE

1. How is sedimentary rock formed from igneous rock? Demonstrate this transformation by repeating the experiment twice, first using yellow and blue paper as in the original experiment, then using white and yellow paper. For ease of handling, work with the paper mulch before it has completely solidified. Break half of the dark mulch into small pieces and press them into a thin layer on top of a stack of newspaper. Make a second layer, using half of the light mulch. Add a third and fourth layer, alternating the dark and light mulches. Allow the model to dry. The two mulches represent two samples of lava. In nature, lava cools and solidifies to form igneous rock. Weathering (the breaking down of rock into smaller pieces by natural processes) causes small

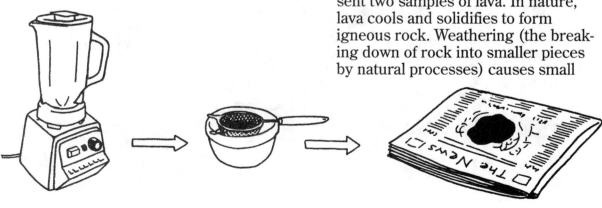

particles of the igneous rock to break off. The particles build up in layers and eventually form sedimentary rock. **Science Fair Hint:** Use the model you made to represent the formation of sedimentary rock.

2. How can metamorphic rock form from sedimentary rock? Demonstrate this transformation by repeating the previous activity. Cover the last layer of mulch with 2 to 3 sheets of newspa- per. In nature, metamorphic rock is formed by pressure applied to rock in solid form. So that you do not have to apply so much pressure, you can work with the layers before they solidify. With a rolling pin, roll back and forth three to four times across the top of the newspaper covering the layers of mulch. Press as hard as you can to try to flatten the layers. Remove the pressed mulch and place it to dry on newspaper. **Science Fair Hint:** Use the model to represent the formation of metamorphic rock.

SHOW TIME!

Rocks come from other rocks. Igneous rock forms when sedimentary or metamorphic rock melts, then cools. Sedimentary rock is made from sediments of metamorphic or igneous rocks. These sediments form as a result of weathering and are deposited in layers. The layers are compacted and cemented. Metamorphic rock forms when igneous or sedimentary rock is changed by heat and/or pressure. This never-ending process by which rocks change from one type to another is called the **rock cycle.** Draw and display a diagram similar to the one shown to represent the rock cycle.

CHECK IT OUT!

1. Each rock type can change into either of the other two rock types. Can a rock be changed into a different rock but remain the same type of rock? For example, can granite, an igneous rock, be heated and cooled to form a different kind of igneous rock? Find out and prepare a display showing different possible changes.

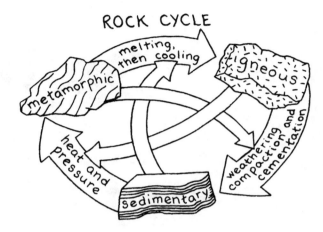

2. Heat and pressure can change granite, an igneous rock, into quartzite, a metamorphic rock. Find out more about the rock cycle. Make diagrams like the one shown, showing the names and types of the rocks and how they change.

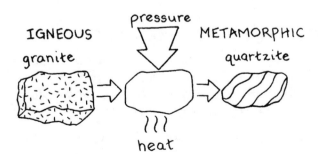

63

16

Splitters

PROBLEM

How can seeds break rocks apart?

Materials

4 tablespoons (60 ml) plaster of paris
two 3-ounce (90-ml) paper cups
tap water
craft stick
4 pinto beans
marking pen
masking tape
2 paper towels

Procedure

*NOTE: Mix the plaster in a throwaway
container. Do not wash the container or
the craft stick in the sink, because the plaster can clog the drain.*

1. Place 2 tablespoons (30 ml) of plaster
in each cup.

2. Add 1 tablespoon (15 ml) of water to
each cup and stir with the craft stick.
Discard the stick.

3. In one of the cups, stand the 4 beans
as far apart as possible on the surface
of the wet plaster. Push the beans into
the plaster so that about three-fourths
of each bean is below the surface of
the plaster.

4. Use the marking pen and tape to label the cup with the beans Test and the cup without beans Control.

5. Record the appearance of the surface of the plaster in each cup.

6. Fold each paper towel in half twice. Wet the folded towels with water so that they are moist but not dripping wet.

7. Push 1 wet towel into each cup until it rests snugly against the surface of the plaster.

8. Place the cups where they will not be disturbed for a week. Wet the towels occasionally to keep them moist.

9. Remove the towels each day for 7 days and record the appearance of the surface of the plaster in each cup. Return the paper towels after each day's observation.

Results

The plaster in the Test cup cracks.

Why?

In this experiment, the plaster in the Control cup does not crack, showing you that it is the growth of the beans that causes the plaster in the Test cup to crack. As the beans grow inside the plaster, they expand, which applies pressure to the plaster. This pressure causes the plaster to crack. The same process can occur when a seed falls into a crack in a rock. The growing seed and its roots push against the rock, forcing the crack to widen and deepen. Eventually the rock can break apart. The breaking down of rock into smaller pieces by natural processes is called weathering. If the rock weathers but there is no change in the chemical composition of the rock, the process is called **physical weathering.**

LET'S EXPLORE

1. Does the size of the mock rock affect the results? Repeat the experiment twice, first using half as much plaster and water, then using twice as much plaster and water. **Science Fair Hint:** Draw diagrams daily of the surface of the plaster. Use the diagrams as part of a project display.

2. Does the amount of water on the surface of the mock rock affect the results? Repeat the original experiment twice. The first time, use dry paper towels instead of wet ones and do not add water. The second time, cover the surface of the plaster with about 1 inch (2.5 cm) of water instead of towels.

3. Do different seeds affect the results? Repeat the original experiment, using different seeds such as those of lima bean, squash, zinnia, and mustard. Test each type of seed separately. For small seeds, push the seeds into the plaster so their surface is level with that of the plaster.

4. Demonstrate the effect of plant roots that move into cracks in rocks by repeating the original experiment, but this time do not press the beans into the surface of the plaster. **Science Fair Hint:** Take photographs each day of the plaster's surface and display them along with textbook photographs of plants growing from split rocks.

5. How does the composition of the mock rock affect the results? Repeat the original experiment, replacing the plaster and water with modeling clay.

SHOW TIME!

Water that seeps into cracks in rocks and freezes can also cause the rocks to split. This occurs because water expands as it freezes. The expanded ice acts as a wedge, widening the crack in the rock. The weathering of rock as a result of repeated freezing and thawing of water is called **frost action.** In time, frost action breaks rocks into smaller and smaller pieces. Demonstrate the expansion and force of water as it freezes by completely filling a drinking straw with water. Plug both ends of the straw with small pieces of modeling clay. Neither plug should extend past the ends of the straw. The water inside the straw should make contact with both clay plugs. Place the straw in a freezer. Observe the position of the clay plugs after 24 hours. Display a diagram showing the position of the clay plugs before and after freezing.

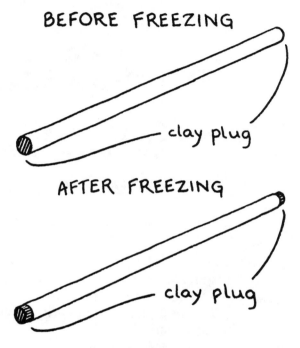

BEFORE FREEZING

clay plug

AFTER FREEZING

clay plug

CHECK IT OUT!

Physical weathering can also be caused by extreme temperature changes. Use an earth science text to find out more about physical weathering. How can burrowing animals such as earthworms, ants, and moles cause rocks to weather? What is exfoliation?

17

Changed

PROBLEM

How does oxygen weather a rock?

Materials

cup
tap water
rubber gloves
lemon-size steel wool pad without
    soap (found at stores that carry
    painting supplies)
saucer
clear plastic drinking glass

Procedure

CAUTION: Steel wool can splinter. Wear rubber gloves when handling steel wool.

1. Half-fill the cup with water.

2. Put on the rubber gloves.

3. Dip the steel wool pad into the cup of water. Hold the steel wool above the cup and allow the excess water to drain into the cup.

4. Place the moistened steel wool on the saucer.

5. Invert the glass and stand it in the saucer so that it covers all of the steel wool.

6. Place the saucer where it will not be disturbed for 5 days.

7. Each day for 5 days, put on the rubber gloves, pick up the steel wool, and rub the wool between your fingers.

Results

Each day, more of the steel wool turns reddish brown and crumbles when touched.

Why?

Oxygen in the air combines with the iron in the steel wool pad to form iron oxide, commonly called **rust.** The rust weakens the structure of the steel wool, causing it to fall apart when touched. Since humidity speeds up the rusting process, the glass in this experiment is used to hold moist air around the steel wool.

The chemical process in which oxygen combines with other substances is called **oxidation.** When oxygen combines with materials in rocks, the compounds formed, such as rust, weaken the structure of the rocks, making them more likely to weather.

Rocks that contain iron often have yellow, orange, or reddish brown colors. Moist air combines with the iron at the surface of these rocks to form iron oxide, and the rocks eventually crumble away as did the steel wool. This breaking down of rock by a change in its chemical composition is called **chemical weathering.**

LET'S EXPLORE

1. Would the iron rust in the same time with no moisture? Repeat the experiment, but this time do not moisten the steel wool.

2. How would **acid rain** (rain with a higher than normal amount of acid) affect the rusting of iron? Acid rain is caused when rain reacts with acid gases from automobile exhausts and factories. Repeat the original experiment, adding ¼ cup (63 ml) of white vinegar to the water. Make observations as often as possible every day for 3 days or until no further changes occur. **Science Fair Hint:** Keep a written record of observations and take photographs of each experiment to show the results as part of a project display.

SHOW TIME!

1. Water can chemically weather rock by dissolving minerals out of the rock. Demonstrate the dissolving effect of

rain on rocks by placing 6 or more sugar cubes, which represent rocks, in a bowl. Place the bowl in a shallow baking pan. Ask an adult to use the point of a pencil to punch three small holes in the bottom of a paper cup, spacing the holes as far apart as possible. Hold your hand over the bottom of the cup while a helper fills it with water, which represents rain. Immediately place the cup about 12 inches (30 cm) above the sugar cubes in the bowl. Remove your hand and observe the effect of the water on the sugar cubes.

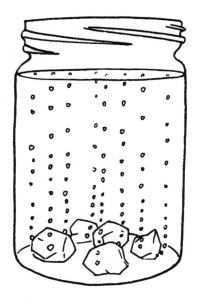

2. Rain chemically weathers all rocks, but usually the change is very slow. Much of the weathering of statues and buildings made of rocks is chemical weathering due to acid rain. Rocks, such as marble, that contain carbonates weather quickly by acid. The acid combines with the carbonate to produce a gas. The weathering of marble by acid rain can be demonstrated by placing marble chips (found at plant nurseries) inside a glass jar. Fill the jar with white vinegar, a mild acid. Observe and record the effect of the acid on the rocks as often as possible

for 1 to 2 days, or until no further changes are seen.

CHECK IT OUT!

Water dissolves more substances than any other liquid. Use an earth science text to find out more about chemical weathering by water. What acid is formed when carbon dioxide in air dissolves in water? What kinds of rock can this acid dissolve? How are caverns created?

18

Splat!

PROBLEM

How do raindrops affect rocks?

Materials

1 teaspoon (5 ml) flour
sheet of black construction paper
eyedropper
tap water
yardstick (meterstick)

Procedure

1. Place the flour in a mound in the center of the paper.

2. Fill the eyedropper with water.

3. Hold the dropper about 12 inches (30 cm) above the center of the flour.

4. Squeeze 2 drops of water onto the mound of flour.

5. Observe the paper.

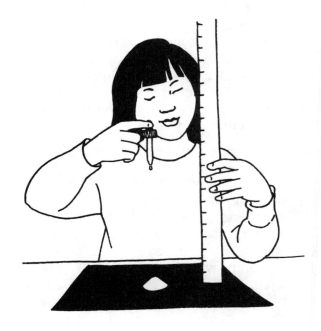

Results

You see a burst of tiny specks of flour on the paper.

Why?

The impact of the falling water forces particles of flour outward. Raindrops hitting the surface of rocks behave similarly to the water drops hitting the flour. Raindrops may fall thousands of yards (thousands of meters) before hitting the ground. The force of the raindrops striking weathered rock can move loosened rock particles.

If rain or other **precipitation** (rain, snow, or other moisture falling from the sky) does not soak into the ground or evaporate, it may form **runoff** (water that flows across land). Runoff picks up and carries away the rock particles loosened by weathering. The moving of rock materials by an **agent of erosion** (something moving, such as water, ice, or wind, that can transport sediment) is called **erosion.** Over a period of time large amounts of rock particles may be eroded.

LET'S EXPLORE

1. Does the distance the water drops fall affect the results? Repeat the experiment twice, first holding the eyedropper about 6 inches (15 cm) above the flour, then placing the paper on the floor and holding the eyedropper about 3 feet (1 m) above the flour.

2. Does particle size affect the results? Repeat the original experiment, replacing the flour with a larger grained material such as cornmeal or sand. **Science Fair Hint:** Take photographs of the construction paper after each experiment and use them to show the results.

SHOW TIME!

1a. **Gravity** is the force that pulls everything toward the center of the earth. Gravity pulls rocks on a sloping surface downhill. Thus, erosion of rocks can be caused by gravity. The movement of earth materials and rock caused by gravity is called **mass wasting.** When rock fragments fall from cliffs or bounce down gentle slopes, they hit other rocks and cause **rock slides** (the sudden downhill sliding of rocks). Demonstrate a rock slide by placing a 6-by-12-inch (15-by-30-cm) piece of cardboard in a baking pan slightly larger than the cardboard. Place

¼ cup (63 ml) of small stones or aquarium gravel in a mound at one end of the cardboard. Slowly raise the mound end of the cardboard about 6 inches (15 cm) or until a few stones slide downhill. Support the cardboard at this height by pressing a block of clay onto the rim of the baking pan. Hold 2 to 3 stones about 12 inches (30 cm) above the mound on the cardboard. Drop the stones.

b. Does the height of the falling stones affect the results? Repeat the previous experiment twice, first holding the stones at a height of 6 inches (15 cm) above the mound, then holding the stones at a height of 2 feet (60 cm).

c. Heavy rain can trigger a rock slide. Demonstrate this by repeating the

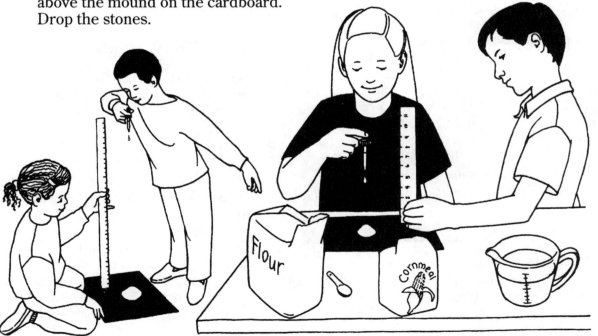

2. Another way erosion occurs is by **abrasion** (a process by which rock is worn away by sediments in an agent of erosion). Sand grains carried by wind, water, and ice can pit and polish the surfaces of rocks. The grains of sand act like a file as they strike and cut away the rocks' surfaces. Simulate abrasion by rubbing a nail file back and forth across a piece of chalk. Prepare a display showing the chalk before and after it was eroded by abrasion.

CHECK IT OUT!

1. The most common way for rock materials to be moved is by gravity. Use earth science texts to find out more about erosion by gravity. What is creep? What type of slope is more likely to produce creep? What is talus?

2. As glaciers move, they drag along rocks. These rocks carried by the glacier scrape against the land, cutting into exposed rocks. Find out more about glacial erosion. What is till? What are the different types of moraine formed by deposits of till?

experiment again, but this time instead of stones, hold a paper cup with water above the mound. While holding the cup, ask an adult to punch two to three holes in the bottom of the cup with a pencil.

19

Rock Record

PROBLEM

What are fossils?

Materials

1-inch (2.5-cm) -thick piece of modeling clay with a surface larger than the shell
petroleum jelly
seashell (or small shell-shaped soap)

Procedure

1. Cover the top surface of the clay with a thin layer of petroleum jelly.

2. Press the outside of the shell firmly into the clay until most of the shell is surrounded by the clay.

3. Gently lift the shell out of the clay.

Results

The shell leaves an impression in the clay.

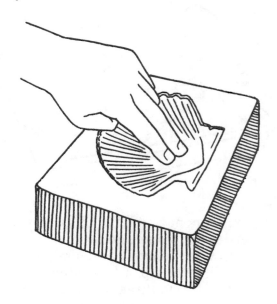

Why?

A **fossil** is any record of past life, such as a shell or a bone preserved in rock. Fossils can also be prints from animals or plants that were made in soft sediment that gradually hardened into solid rock. Fossils were and can be made from the remains of an **organism** (any living thing, such as plants or animals) buried in sediment. The remains rot away completely as the sediment hardens into rock, leaving in the rock a cavity the size and shape of the organism. This impression of an organism within a rock cavity is called a **fossil mold.**

This experiment represents the formation of a fossil mold. The shell represents the remains of the organism, and the clay represents the soft sediment that will harden into rock. The print left by the shell is a model of a fossil mold.

LET'S EXPLORE

1. The cavity in which an object can be shaped is called a **mold.** A fossil mold can be used as a mold to create a reproduction of the surface texture of the organism. Repeat the experiment, making another impression of the shell. In a paper cup, mix 2 tablespoons (30 ml) of plaster of paris with 1 tablespoon (15 ml) of tap water, then stir with a craft stick. Fill this mold with the wet plaster. Allow the plaster to dry (about 20 to 30 minutes), then remove the clay. The dried plaster retains the actual surface texture of the original object, the shell. *NOTE: Do not wash the paper cup or the craft*

stick in the sink, because the plaster can clog the drain.

2. Under the right conditions in nature, mud that fills fossil molds will harden and retain the shape of the mold. When a mold is filled with a substance such as mud or plaster that hardens, the result is a solid reproduction of an organism, called a **cast.** Casts have the same outer shape as the organism. Mud casts that change into rock form fossil prints of the organism. Make a mud cast by repeating the previous experiment, but replace the plaster with garden soil. **Science Fair Hint:** Use the mold and cast of the shell as part of a science fair display.

SHOW TIME!

1. Another way to show how fossil molds form in sedimentary rock is by mixing together ½ cup (125 ml) flour, ½ cup (125 ml) cornmeal, and ½ cup (125 ml) tap water in a bowl. Pour this "home-made mud" onto a paper plate. Spread the fingers of one of your hands, and press that hand palm side down into the mud. Lift your hand. You should see a good print of your hand in the mud. Place the paper plate near a window where it will receive direct sunlight and will not be disturbed. Allow several days for the mud to dry. Display photographs of the procedure and the results to represent the formation of a mold.

2. How does metamorphism affect fossils? Use the fossil mold model made in the previous experiment to represent how pressure changes sedimentary rock into metamorphic rock. Roll a rolling pin back and forth across the hardened mold. Take photographs of the mold before and after applying pressure, and use them to prepare a poster representing the effects of metamorphism. The title of the poster might be "Fossils versus Metamorphism." See chapter 13, "Recycled Rock," for more information about metamorphism.

CHECK IT OUT!

1. Fossils are more commonly found in limestone and shale than in sandstone. Find out more about fossils and the

rocks in which they are found. Why are fossils found in sedimentary rock but not in igneous or metamorphic rock? What is fossiliferous limestone?

2. Petrified wood forms when silica minerals in groundwater replace wood fibers and/or fill pores in buried wood. Find out more about this process. How long does it take for complete petrification? Where is petrified wood of gem quality found?

20

Collection

PROBLEM

How do you label a mineral collection?

Materials

mineral samples (found in your area or purchased from local rock and mineral shops or teaching supply stores. See Appendix for other sources.)
white typewriter correcting fluid with brush
timer
black fine-point permanent marking pen
2 index cards for each mineral sample
2 card file boxes

Procedure

1. Label each mineral sample by using the following steps:

- With the brush, paint a small spot of correcting fluid on each mineral sample. Place the spot in an unimportant area on the mineral.
- Wait 2 to 3 minutes to allow the spot to dry.
- Write a reference number on each spot.

2. Prepare a card file by using the following steps:
   - Write the reference number of each mineral sample on a file card.
   - Write the details of each sample, including the following:
     a. specimen's name
     b. where it was obtained (If found in nature, include information about other minerals or rocks at the location.)
     c. identifying features, such as color, luster (shininess), hard-

ness, cleavage, and streak
- Place the cards in one of the card file boxes in numerical order.
- Prepare a second set of cards with identical information, but place the cards in the other card file box in alphabetical order.

Results

You've created an index card catalog of a mineral collection.

Why?

The numbered minerals and the set of numerically ordered index cards make it easy for you to quickly identify each sample in your mineral collection. The second set of cards in alphabetical order allows you to search by name for a specific mineral in your collection and its corresponding reference number.

LET'S EXPLORE

1a. How do you label a rock collection? Repeat the procedure for labeling minerals, but use rock samples and a different color of correcting fluid.

b. Along with the reference number, place a letter on each rock to identify its class. Use the following letter identification system or design your own: S—sedimentary, M—metamorphic, I—igneous.

2. If you wish to keep your fossil collection separate from the rest of your rock collection, repeat the original procedure for labeling minerals, but use fossil samples and a third color of correcting fluid.

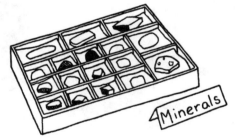

SHOW TIME!

1. Store your rock and mineral collections in a way that keeps the samples separate from one another. Place the samples in egg cartons or in small boxes arranged on a tray, shallow box, or baking pan. Put cotton beneath each specimen as padding. Place all your rock samples in one carton or on one tray, all your mineral samples in another carton or tray, and use a third carton or tray if you prefer to keep fossil samples separate. Identify your collections with stand-up signs made from index cards folded in half lengthwise and labeled Rocks, Minerals, and Fossils if included.

2. Use a wooden backboard with shelves on each panel as a project display. Display individual samples with an information card stating important and/or interesting facts about the sample, such as its name, where you found it, and its use. Mention identifying tests, such as hardness and streak tests, on the card. List each mineral's specific gravity and cleavage tendencies. Make some samples of rocks and minerals available so that observers can touch and feel them. Be prepared to answer observers' questions about any and all samples displayed.

CHECK IT OUT!

1. Every geographic location has its own natural collection of rocks and minerals. Check with the geology depart-

ment of nearby colleges, universities, and/or high schools for information about local rocks and minerals. Those educational institutions may also be able to provide locations of rock and mineral shops in your area.

2. Use the library to find available rock and mineral books, magazines, and articles. *Rocks & Minerals* magazine is a wonderful resource. See the Appendix for additional resources.

Appendix

Books

Chesterman, Charles W. *The Audubon Society Field Guide to North American Rocks and Minerals.* New York: Alfred A. Knopf, 1979.

Cvancara, Alan. *A Field Manual for the Amateur Geologist,* rev. ed. New York: John Wiley & Sons, 1995.

Dixon, Dougal. *The Practical Geologist.* New York: Simon & Schuster, 1992.

Lambert, David. *The Field Guide to Geology.* New York: Facts on File, 1989.

Oliver, Ray. *Rocks & Fossils.* New York: Random House, 1993.

Pellant, Chris. *Rocks and Minerals.* New York: Dorling Kindersley, 1992.

Rowland-Entwistle, Theodore, and Michael O'Donoghue. *Rocks & Minerals.* San Diego: Thunder Bay Press, 1994.

VanCleave, Janice. *Janice VanCleave's Earth Science for Every Kid.* New York: John Wiley & Sons, 1991.

Zike, Dinah. *The Earth Science Book: Activities for Kids.* New York: John Wiley & Sons, 1992.

Catalog Suppliers of Rocks and Minerals

Carolina Biological Supply Company
2700 York Road
Burlington, NC 27215
(800) 334-5551

Connecticut Valley Biological Company
82 Valley Road
P.O. Box 326
Southampton, MA 01073
(800) 628-7748

Edmund Scientific Company
101 East Gloucester Pike
Barrington, NJ 08007
(609) 547-3488

Fisher Scientific
Educational Materials Division
485 South Frontage Road
Burr Ridge, IL 60521
(708) 655-4410
(800) 766-7000

Frey Scientific Company
905 Hickory Lane
Mansfield, OH 44905
(419) 589-2100

Geoscience Industries
225 Smokey Street
Fort Collins, CO 80525
(303) 223-5511

NASCO
901 Janesville Avenue
P.O. Box 901
Fort Atkinson, WI 53538
(800) 677-2960

Nevada Mineral & Book Company
4728 Elm Avenue
Las Vegas, NV 89110
(702) 453-5718

Sargent-Welch
911 Commerce Court
Buffalo Grove, IL 60089
(800) 727-4368

Ward's Natural Science
5100 West Henrietta Road
Rochester, NY 14586
(800) 962-2660

Other Sources of Rocks and Minerals

The following stores carry rocks and minerals and are located in many areas. To find the stores near you, call the home offices listed below.

Nature Company
750 Hearst Avenue
Berkeley, CA 94701
(800) 227-1114

Nature of Things
10700 West Venture Drive
Franklin, WI 53132-2804
(800) 283-2921

The Discovery Store
15046 Beltway Drive
Dallas, TX 75244
(214) 490-8299

World of Science
900 Jefferson Road
Building 4
Rochester, NY 14623
(716) 475-0100

Glossary

abrasion   The process by which rock is worn away by sediments in an agent of erosion.

acid rain   Rain with a higher than normal amount of acid; caused when rain reacts with acid gases from automobile exhausts and factories.

agent of erosion   Something moving, such as water, ice, or wind, that can transport sediment.

atom   The building unit of matter; the smallest part of an element that retains the properties of the element.

calcite   The most common carbonate; has a hardness of 3, cleaves perfectly in three different directions, is usually whitish or colorless, and has a white to grayish streak.

carbonate   A mineral containing combinations of carbon and oxygen and some other element, such as calcium, barium, or manganese.

cast   A solid reproduction of an organism, having the same outer shape as the organism, which is made by filling a mold with a substance such as mud or plaster that hardens.

cementation   The process by which minerals dissolved in water cement sediment together during the formation of sedimentary rock.

chemical compound   A combination of two or more different elements.

chemical particles   Atoms and molecules.

chemical weathering   The breaking down of rock as a result of changes in its chemical composition.

cleavage   The tendency of a mineral to break along a smooth surface.

cleavage plane   The area of a mineral where it can be easily split apart.

cohesion   The attraction between like chemical particles.

common streak test   The act of rubbing a mineral against a streak plate to determine the mineral's streak.

compaction   The process by which layers of sediment are squeezed together during the formation of sedimentary rock.

compress   To squeeze closer together.

crust   The relatively thin outermost layer of the earth.

crystal   A solid made up of atoms arranged in an orderly, regular pattern; a recognizable shape that results from the repetition of the same combination of atomic particles.

cubic   Shaped like a box, having six equal, square sides that are at right angles to each other.

displace   To push out of place.

dripstones   The common name for stalactites and stalagmites.

element   Matter that is made of only one kind of atom.

erosion   The process by which rock materials are worn away by abrasion or by which sediments are moved by an agent of erosion.

evaporate   To change from a liquid to a gas.

fluid   Capable of flowing; also a substance in the liquid or gas phase.

foliated rock   Metamorphic rock with layers.

fossil A record or the traces of past life, such as impressions of or a shell, bone, or other hard part of an animal or plant, preserved in rock.

fossil mold An impression of an organism within a rock cavity.

fracture A way in which a mineral breaks other than along a smooth surface; uneven breaking.

frost action The weathering of rock as a result of repeated freezing and thawing of water.

gas A phase of matter with no definite volume or shape.

gravity The force that pulls everything toward the center of the earth.

gypsum A soft mineral that has a hardness of 2, monoclinic-shaped crystals and is made of calcium sulfate.

halite The mineral called common salt or table salt.

hardness A mineral's resistance to being scratched.

humidity The amount of water in the air.

igneous rock Rock formed when hot liquid rock cools and hardens.

inorganic Used to describe substances not formed from the remains of living organisms.

lava Magma that reaches the earth's surface.

limestone A sedimentary rock made wholly or chiefly of calcium carbonate.

liquid A phase of matter with a definite volume but no definite shape.

lithosphere The solid part of the earth, made up of crust and the upper part of the mantle.

lodestone "Leading stone;" common name for magnetite.

magma Liquid rock beneath the earth's surface.

magnetic domain A cluster of atoms organized so that one side of the cluster is attracted to the earth's magnetic north pole and the other side is attracted to the earth's magnetic south pole.

magnetite A mineral that contains a high percentage of iron and behaves like a magnet; also called lodestone.

magnetized The condition in which the magnetic domains in a magnetic material, such as iron, line up so that their north-seeking sides point in the same direction.

mantle The inner layer of the earth beneath the crust.

mass The amount of material in an object.

mass wasting The movement of earth materials and rock caused by gravity.

matter Anything that takes up space and has mass.

melting point The temperature at which a solid changes to a liquid.

metamorphic rock Rock that forms from other types of rock by pressure and heat.

metamorphism The process of changing one rock type to another by pressure and heat.

mineral A single, solid element or chemical compound found in the earth that makes up rock and that has four basic characteristics: (1) it occurs naturally; (2) it is inorganic; (3) it has a definite chemical composition; and (4) it has a crystalline structure.

mold A cavity in which an object can be shaped.

molecule The smallest part of a compound that retains the properties of the compound and that is made up of atoms held together by chemical bonds.

nonfoliated rock Metamorphic rock without layers.

organic Used to describe substances formed from living matter.

organism Any living thing such as plants, animals, fungi or microbes.

oxidation The chemical process by which oxygen combines with other substances.

physical weathering The breaking down of rock without any changes in its chemical composition.

pole Either end of a bar magnet or of an imaginary axis that passes through the center of the earth.

precipitation Rain, snow, or other moisture falling from the sky.

right angle An angle that measures 90 degrees.

rock A solid made up of one or more minerals.

rock cycle The never-ending process by which rocks change from one type to another.

rock formers The abundant minerals that make up the bulk of the lithosphere.

rock slides A sudden downhill sliding of rocks.

runoff Water that flows across land.

rust Iron oxide, formed when iron oxidizes.

sediment Small particles of material, such as bits of rock, shells, or the remains of a plant or animal, deposited by wind, water, or ice.

sedimentary rock Rock formed by deposits of sediment.

solid A phase of matter with a definite shape and a definite volume.

specific gravity The ratio of the mass of a substance, such as a mineral, in air compared to the mass of an equal volume of water; calculated by dividing the mass of the substance by the mass of the water displaced by the substance.

stalactites Calcium carbonate deposits hanging from the roof or walls of a cave or cavern.

stalagmites Calcium carbonate deposits projecting up from the floor of a cave or cavern.

streak The color of the powder left when a mineral is rubbed against a rough surface that is harder than the mineral.

streak plate The surface of unglazed porcelain or other material against which a mineral is rubbed in a common streak test.

tetragonal Shaped like a rectangular shoe box or like a cube, but with a pyramid at the top and bottom.

three-dimensional Having three measurements—height, width, and length.

viscosity The property of a liquid that makes it resistant to flow.

weathering The breaking down of rock into smaller pieces by natural processes.

xenolith A piece of solid rock mixed with magma.

zircon A mineral with a hardness of 7½ and tetragonal-shaped crystals.

ndex

Get these fun and exciting books by Janice VanCleave

at your local bookstore, call toll-free 1-800-225-5945, or
fill out the order form below and mail to:
John Wiley & Sons, Inc., Order Processing Department, 432 Elizabeth Ave.
Somerset, New Jersey   08875

Visit our Website at: www.wiley.com

Over 2 million sold!

Janice VanCleave's Science Fair for Every Kid Series

__Astronomy	53573-7	$12.95 US / $19.95 CAN
__Biology	50381-9	$11.95 US / $17.95 CAN
__Chemistry	62085-8	$12.95 US / $19.95 CAN
__Constellations	15979-4	$12.95 US / $19.95 CAN
__Dinosaurs	30812-9	$10.95 US / $16.95 CAN
__Earth Science	53010-7	$12.95 US / $19.95 CAN
__Ecology	10086-2	$10.95 US / $16.95 CAN
__Food/ Nutrition	17665-6	$12.95 US / $19.95 CAN
__Geography	59842-9	$12.95 US / $19.95 CAN
__Geometry	31141-3	$12.95 US / $19.95 CAN
__Human Body	02408-2	$12.95 US / $19.95 CAN
__Math	54265-2	$12.95 US / $19.95 CAN
__Oceans	12453-2	$12.95 US / $19.95 CAN
__Physics	52505-7	$12.95 US / $19.95 CAN

Janice VanCleave's Science Bonanzas

__200 Gooey, Slippery, Slimy, Weird & Fun Experiments
    57921-1 $12.95 US / $19.95 CAN
__201 Awesome, Magical, Bizarre, & Incredible Experiments
    31011-5 $12.95 US / $19.95 CAN
__202 Oozing, Bubbling, Dripping & Bouncing Experiments
    14025-2 $12.95 US / $19.95 CAN
__203 Icy, Freezing, Frosty, Cool & Wild Experiments
    25223-9 $12.95 US / $19.95 CAN

Janice VanCleave's Spectacular Science Projects

__Animals	55052-3	$10.95 US / $16.95 CAN
__Earthquakes	57107-5	$10.95 US / $16.95 CAN
__Electricity	31010-7	$10.95 US / $16.95 CAN
__Gravity	55050-7	$10.95 US / $16.95 CAN
__Insects/Spiders	16396-1	$10.95 US / $16.95 CAN
__Machines	57108-3	$10.95 US / $16.95 CAN
__Magnets	57106-7	$10.95 US / $16.95 CAN
__Microscopes & Magnifying Lenses	58956-X	$10.95 US / $16.95 CAN
__Molecules	55054-X	$10.95 US / $16.95 CAN
__Plants	14687-0	$10.95 US / $16.95 CAN
__Rocks and Minerals	10269-5	$10.95 US / $16.95 CAN
__Solar System	32204-0	$10.95 US / $16.95 CAN
__Volcanoes	30811-0	$10.95 US / $16.95 CAN
__Weather	03231-X	$10.95 US / $16.95 CAN

Janice VanCleave's A+ Projects Series

__Biology	58628-5	$12.95 US / $19.95 CAN
__Chemistry	58630-7	$12.95 US / $19.95 CAN
__Earth Science	17770-9	$12.95 US / $19.95 CAN

WILEY
Independent Thinkers

- -

[ ] Check/Money order enclosed. Please include your local sales tax and $5.00 for handling charges.
[ ] Charge my: [ ]VISA   [ ]MASTERCARD   [ ]AMERICAN EXPRESS [ ]DISCOVER
Card #:_____. Expiration Date:_____
SIGNATURE:_____(Offer not valid unless signed)
NAME:_____
ADDRESS:_____
CITY_____STATE_____ ZIP_____

Prices subject to change without notice.